better together*

*This book is best read together, grownup and kid.

 akidsco.com

a kids
book
about

a kids book about

NERVOUS SYSTEM SYSTEM REGULATION

by Dr. Joy Malik-Hasbrook

a
kids
book
about

Printed in the United States of America.

A Kids Book About books are available online: *akidsco.com*

To share your stories, ask questions, or inquire about bulk
purchases (schools, libraries, and nonprofits), please use
the following email address: *hello@akidsco.com*

ISBN: 978-1-958825-19-8

Designed by Rick DeLucco
Edited by Emma Wolf

The author would like to acknowledge and thank Stephen W. Porges, Ph.D.,
and his inspiring work on Polyvagal Theory.

1. Green, red, and blue nervous system regulation color identification system: Adapted from Infant/Child Mental Health, Early Intervention,
and Relationship-Based Therapies: A Neurorelational Framework for Interdisciplinary Practice by Connie Lillas & Janiece Turnbull © 2009 by
Interdisciplinary Training Institute LLC and Janiece Turnbull, was used with permission from the publisher W.W. Norton & Company, Inc.
2. "Concentric Circles" illustration and text from "Anchored" © 2021 Deborah A. Dana, was used with permission from the publisher, Sounds True, Inc.

To John, Wylie, and Lola—you inspire me
and fill my heart full of green energy.

To the women who keep me going
and to all the women who bravely share
their stories and wisdom—thank you.

Intro

Let's pause for a moment and take a breath. Put one hand on your heart and one on your stomach and picture someone who warms your heart. Let your mind be filled with this thought: I am enough and I am not alone.

Can you feel yourself settle?

This is your nervous system regulating, which is not always easy to do. As grownups, we are under constant pressure to care for others and manage many stressors, all of which tax our nervous system.

Similarly, kids can become easily overwhelmed because their brains are still developing, and they are constantly adapting and processing so much. They show us their dysregulation through behaviors like screaming for no apparent reason, trying to control everything, or being totally disengaged. Our nervous system is wired to feel safe when we feel like we belong, so these are cues that they feel disconnected, overwhelmed, or scared. What they need most is connection.

When I was a kid, there was
a lot of yelling in my house.

When things got really loud,
I felt a wave of worry
and ran to my room.

I didn't understand why
my parents were so upset or
what was going on in my body.

Now that I'm a grownup,
I know this has a lot to do with
my nervous system regulation.

WHAT IS THE NERVOUS SYSTEM?

Our nervous system is made up of the brain, spine, and other parts of our body.

It guides so much of what we do, like:

BREATHING,

 FEELING,

 THINKING,

 MOVING,

 DIGESTING,

 AND IT PROTECTS US.

Our amazing nervous system takes care of these things every day without us realizing it!

The nervous system is our survival mechanism from when our ancestors lived in the wild, which protected them from threats like other animals.

Its job is still to keep us alive and monitor our safety, but the triggers we face today are different and can include:

- BEING BULLIED, YELLED AT, OR TALKED DOWN TO,

- EXPERIENCING INJUSTICE,

- YOUR BODY EXPERIENCING SICKNESS, HUNGER, OR EXTREME TIREDNESS,

- FEELING LIKE YOU'RE NOT GOOD ENOUGH,

- FEELING CONFUSED,

- OR FEELING DIFFERENT AND EXCLUDED.

Have you experienced any
of those triggers before?

Believe me,

YOU ARE N

OT ALONE.

When something makes us feel disconnected, overwhelmed, or scared, our nervous system may get

DYSREGULATED.

When we are dysregulated, we can't think or respond like we normally do.

Instead, our nervous system reacts so quickly we aren't even aware of it.

When we are dysregulated, our nervous system **REACTS** from our survival brain and not our thinking brain.*

*Scientists call this action our "stress" or "survival" response.

Figure 1

Prefrontal Cortex
(your Thinking Brain)

Limbic System
(your Survival Brain)

The main survival responses are...

FIGHT/FLIGHT

OR

FREEZE.

Fight/flight is also called the "red" response, which is when we feel super mad or scared and we may want to criticize, yell, or hit (fight), or run away (flight).

In the red response, our nervous system is activated with lots of energy, and all the stress we're feeling wants to leave our body to make things safer.

The other survival response (freeze) is also called the "blue" response, which is when we feel lonely, really tired, or like disappearing.

In the blue response, our nervous system doesn't have enough energy and tries to protect us by turning the stress inward and shutting down.

Sometimes kids describe the red as feeling like their body is super hot and going too fast!

And the blue can feel as if your body is frozen like ice and moving so slowly.

Which words describe how the red and blue responses feel for you?

Grownups, how do they
feel in your body?

When we get dysregulated,
we might think,

"Is there something wrong with me?"

The answer is **ABSOLUTELY NOT!**

This is part of being human.

So, what makes our nervous system feel safe and **REGULATED?**

Feeling like we **BELONG.**

We are able to regulate when we feel connected with each other and ourselves.

Being regulated is also called the "green" response, which is when we feel safe and connected.

Our brain and body are working together as a team—we need all 3 of these responses to work together in order for us to thrive.

Figure 2

Safe/Connected   Fight/Flight   Freeze

Don't get me wrong—being regulated doesn't mean you never have big feelings, get upset, or have difficult things happen!

 IT MEANS WE CAN BE BRAVE, EVEN WHEN WE'RE SCARED.

 WE CAN KEEP GOING, EVEN WHEN THINGS FEEL HARD.

 WE CAN HAVE EMPATHY AND HELP SOMEONE ELSE.

Our energy moves through these different responses all day.

When the green, blue, and red work together we can learn, play, and rest.

Not having enough moments of green
causes us to be dysregulated.

When this happens, how can we return to regulation and feel more green energy?

Well, it supports your
nervous system a lot when
a regulated grownup is there to
help you in your stress response.

Their green energy helps regulate
your red or blue energy.

Other things that calm our nervous systems are:

- SLOWLY BREATHING WITH SOMEONE OR ON YOUR OWN

- NAMING THE COLOR YOU ARE IN

- TELLING YOURSELF, "I'M OK. AND EVERYTHING IS OK RIGHT NOW."

- MOVING YOUR BODY

- LISTENING TO MUSIC

- LAUGHING OR CRYING, WHICH RELEASES STRESS

- WRITING OR DRAWING

Some people need to take a break and get some space

(I've learned my nervous system needs lots of breaks, especially when I hear yelling).

Other people don't want space and need tight hugs.

What works for your nervous system or what do you want to try?

Grownups, what about you?

Regulation is something we practice every day.

But there will still be times when we react from our stress responses in ways we might regret.

So, what do we do when that happens?

WE REPAIR.

This means having compassion for each other and for ourselves.

If we do something hurtful while in a stress response, once we are regulated, we can say something like, "I'm sorry, I was in the red. How can I make this better?"

Repairing also helps our green response get stronger!

In any situation, you can talk to yourself in a kind way.

When you do this, it's like your green energy is hugging your blue and red responses.

Figure 3

I wish that when I was a kid, my family and I were taught nervous system regulation.

My parents' stress wasn't my fault.

Their nervous systems were dysregulated, and that affected my own ability to regulate.

So, my hope is that this book
helps you and your grownups
build your green energy together.

What if more families
and schools did this?

If we all worked to create a

COLLE

CTIVE

green response together, just imagine what we could do to make the world a better place for everyone.

Outro

Regulating ourselves is the most important thing we can do to help kids learn how to regulate themselves. Over time, kids build their nervous system regulation through having grownups respond to them with empathy, attunement, and respectful boundaries.

But we cannot co-regulate if we are dysregulated.

Our nervous system is also designed to remember past feelings of threat to try to protect us. Kids have a remarkable way of unconsciously mirroring back to us our past stress and wounds that we have not fully processed. These things tax and trigger our nervous system.

This is a call to heal and use our own green energy to hug the red or blue distress we experience. To answer this call, I invite you to understand your own nervous system—what triggers it and what helps you return to regulation. And may this journey be guided by self-care, compassion, community, resiliency, and lots of repair!

About The Author

Dr. Joy Malik-Hasbrook, PsyD (she/her), is a psychologist who helps children feel seen and grownups heal. She gives presentations on regulation and resiliency-based parenting, specializes in neurodiversity assessments with kids, and is a leader at a nonprofit counseling center.

She is a mama of 2, a highly sensitive human, and biracial of South Asian Indian/white descent. She values integrating both Asian contemplative practices and contemporary psychology into her work.

Dr. Joy understands how challenges with dysregulation create more distress, pulling on experiences from her own childhood, as a mother, or from the families she supports. She believes that understanding nervous system regulation leads to compassion and resiliency and that all families should have access to this information—this book is a start!

 @dr.joy_compassionateparenting 🌐 drjoymalikhasbrook.com

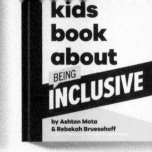

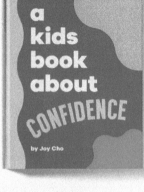

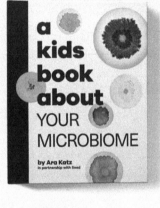

Printed in the USA
CPSIA information can be obtained
at www.ICGtesting.com
LVHW071557301023
762359LV00088B/180

9 781958 825198